MOVING ART

Hilary Devonshire

Consultant: Henry Pluckrose

Photography: Chris Fairclough

FRANKLIN WATTS
London/New York/Sydney/Toronto

Copyright © 1990 Franklin Watts

Franklin Watts
96-98 Leonard Street
London EC2A 4RH

Franklin Watts Australia
14 Mars Road
Lane Cove
NSW 2066

UK ISBN: 0 7496 0142 6

Design: K & Co

Editor: Jenny Wood

Typeset by Lineage Ltd,
Watford, England

Printed in Belgium

Contents

Equipment and materials

This book describes activities which use the following:

Adhesives – clear cold water paste (e.g. wallpaper paste), acrylic PVA
Beads
Bottle (with its cork)
Brushes (for glue and paint)
Card (thin white and coloured card, and thick card)
Cardboard boxes
Cardboard tubes
Craft knife
Crayons
Dowel rod
Elastic bands
Fabric (soft, thin material e.g. nylon, polyester, silk, and assorted scraps)
Felt-tip pens (a selection of colours)
Garden sticks
Hole punch
Junk materials (e.g. assorted waste packaging)
Masking tape
Matchboxes
Modelling clay (e.g. Plasticine)
Needle
Newspaper (old)

Paint (acrylic, poster or powder)
Pair of compasses
Paper (white and coloured)
Paper fasteners
Paper plates
Pastels (oil)
Pencil
Ping-pong ball
Pin (long)
Plastic bowl (an old one, for mixing papier mâché)
Plates (one large, one small, for drawing round)
Ribbons
Ruler (wooden or plastic, and metal for use with the craft knife)
Scissors
Sequins
Sticky tape
String (thin)
Thread (e.g. cotton thread or embroidery silk)
Tray (round)
Wool
Wrapping paper (patterned)
Yoghurt cartons

Getting ready

Getting ready

I decided to call this book *Moving Art* because in each model or design there is some part which moves, or gives the impression of movement. Some of the ideas described are optical illusions, a trick of the eye. Others are three-dimensional and therefore more lifelike.

Action or movement in a picture or model can make it much more exciting. You can also use the action or movement to create a surprise within the picture or model – see, for example, the pop-up figure on pages 20-23.

The card or toy that you make could be a present for a friend or relative. You could surprise them too!

When you have experimented with the ideas in this book and discovered how the movement occurs, try to use the techniques to develop new models and designs of your own. Turning an idea into something new is being truly creative. Have fun!

1 Important pieces of equipment.

A rocking design

You will need some thin white card, a pen or pencil, a round tray, crayons, PVA glue and a glue brush.

1 Place your tray on the white card and draw round part of the rim to make the curved base for your picture.

2 Draw your picture and colour it in.

3 Cut out another piece of card with a matching curved base. This will be the support that will allow your picture to stand up. Draw a line 1cm from the top edge.

4 Fold along this line and brush glue along the edge.

5 Fix the card support to the back of your picture so that the two base edges are parallel.

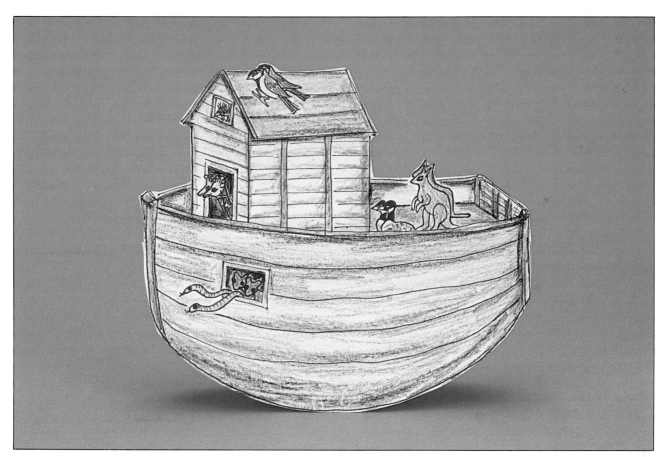

6 *Noah's Ark* Push the Ark and watch it rock.

Here are some ideas for other rocking designs:
a) a balancing juggler,
b) a swimming duck,
c) a rocking cradle.

A rotating scene

In this scene you will be able to change the weather from sun to snow! You will need three pieces of thin white card (A4), a pencil, a ruler, a pair of compasses, scissors, paints, paintbrushes, a paper fastener, PVA glue and a glue brush.

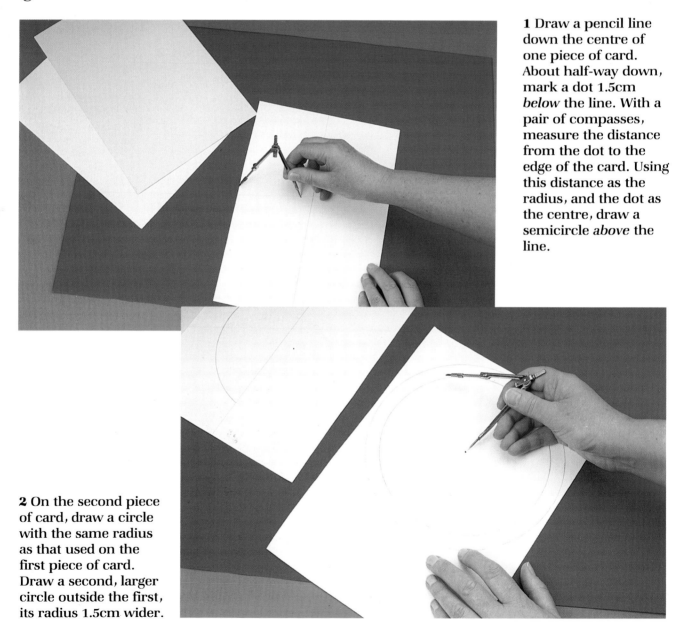

1 Draw a pencil line down the centre of one piece of card. About half-way down, mark a dot 1.5cm *below* the line. With a pair of compasses, measure the distance from the dot to the edge of the card. Using this distance as the radius, and the dot as the centre, draw a semicircle *above* the line.

2 On the second piece of card, draw a circle with the same radius as that used on the first piece of card. Draw a second, larger circle outside the first, its radius 1.5cm wider.

3 Draw a sun in one half of the inner circle and snowflakes in the other half. Cut out your circle, around the outer edge.

4 Draw a scene around the semicircle on the first piece of card...

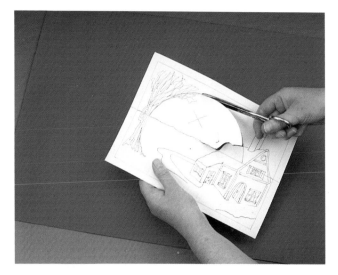

5 ...then cut away the semicircular space.

6 Paint your scene. Paint the sky and sun in the circle, too, adding a decorative border if you like.

7 Push the paper fastener through the dot below the line...

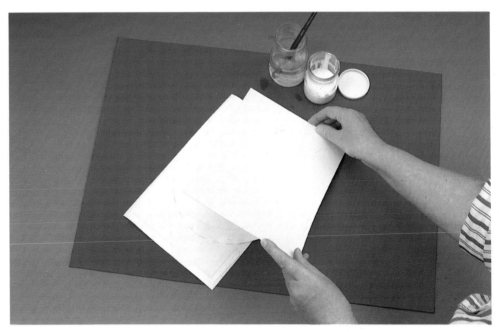

8 ...then through the centre of the circle and, finally, through a spare piece of card cut to a square. Open out the fastener.

9 Glue around the paper fastener on the square piece of card and also around the edges of the back of your picture.

10 Mount your picture on to the third piece of card. Press firmly and leave to dry.

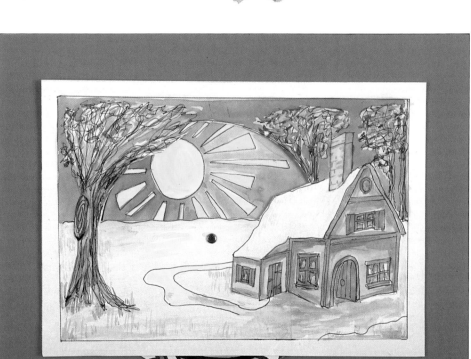

11 The card circle will rotate inside the scene. Here the sun is shining...

12 ...and here the snow has started to fall!

When the frog's mouth opens and shuts, it appears to be talking. You can design fun greetings cards using this idea.

You will need paper, crayons, scissors, glue and some heavy paper or card for mounting.

1 Draw and colour your frog (or any creature of your choice). Make sure your drawing is as symmetrical as possible, on either side of the centre of the paper.

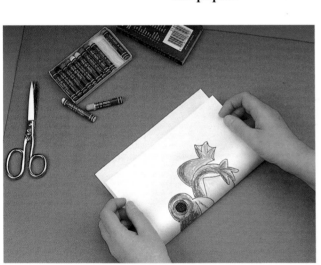

2 Keeping the picture of the frog on the outside, fold the paper in half and...

3 ...cut along the line of the frog's mouth.

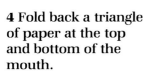

4 Fold back a triangle of paper at the top and bottom of the mouth.

5 Open out your picture then fold it in half again, this time with the frog on the inside. Push the folded triangles of the mouth forward.

6 Close the paper and press firmly along the folds of the mouth (which are now folded back inside).

7 You can experiment with different lengths of cuts and larger triangular folds. Some mouths will open wide, others will be like small beaks.

8 Stick your frog on to a piece of thick card (or heavy paper) folded along the centre.

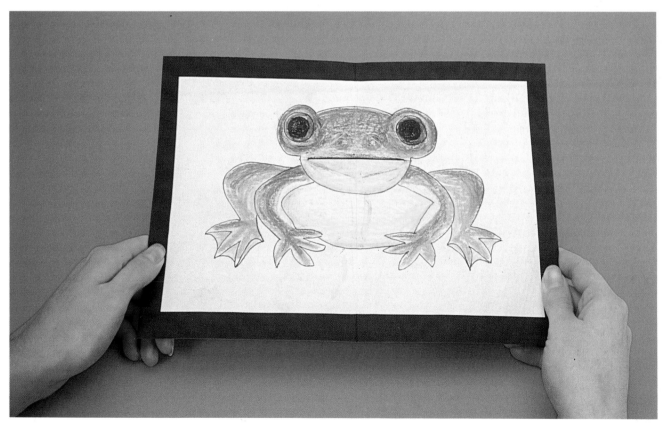

9 As you open and close the card, the frog's mouth will open and shut. The owl in the background has a moving, pointed beak made in the same way.

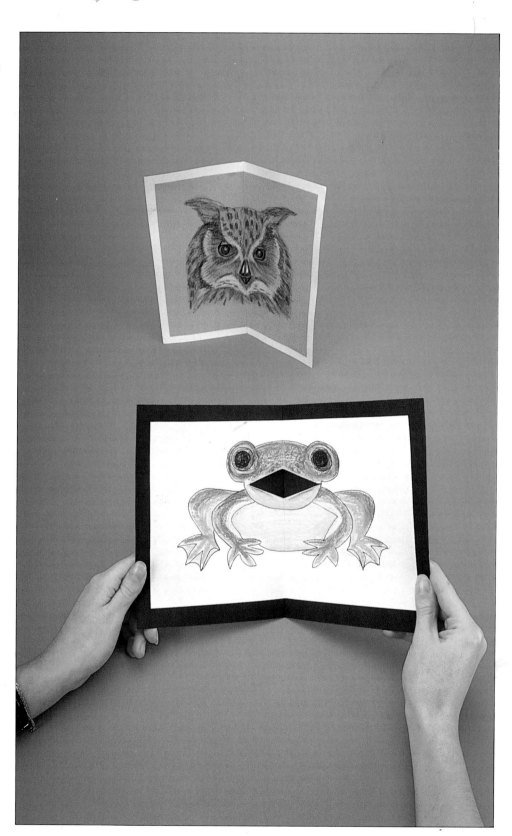

Make a character with moving arms, or a bird with flapping wings! You will need thin white cardboard, a pencil, felt-tip pens, scissors, two paper fasteners, a needle, embroidery thread and a bead.

1 Draw the body of your character on a piece of card. Draw the two arms separately. Colour your figure with felt-tip pens.

2 Cut out your figure and loosely attach the arms at the shoulders with the two paper fasteners.

3 Using the needle, thread a length of embroidery thread through the top of the arms above the paper fasteners.

4 With the arms hanging straight down, tie the thread so that it is tight across the back of the figure. Leave a long piece of thread to use as a pull. Tie a bead on the end of the thread.

5 *The Pirate* The finished figure.

6 When you pull the thread, the pirate will raise his arms. The second figure shown here was created from a sketch drawn in a museum. Can you make a figure which moves both arms *and* legs?

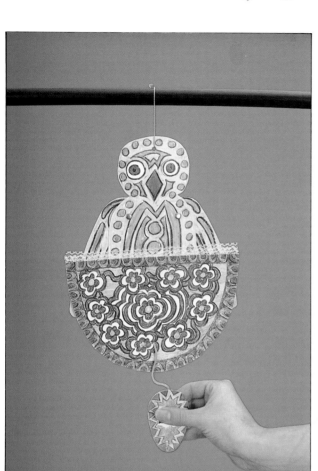

7 Here is another idea.
A decorated chick...

8 ...bursts from its
egg!

Pop-up art – a pop-up figure

Pop-up designs are a popular way of making cards which contain a surprise when they are opened. For this idea you will need thin white card, felt-tip pens, scissors, a small quantity of PVA glue and a glue brush.

1 Draw a figure (a person or creature) on a postcard-size piece of card.

2 Make a single triangular opening in the fold of an A4 piece of card. (Follow the instructions for the frog on page 13.)

3 Draw and cut a triangle at one end of a strip of card, to match the fold in the card.

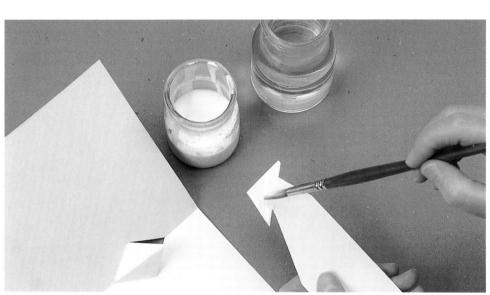

4 Glue the triangle then...

5 ...stick it firmly to the fold. Leave to dry.

6 The strip will move down as you close the card.

7 Fold the card and...

8 ...cut off the piece of card strip which sticks out when the card is closed.

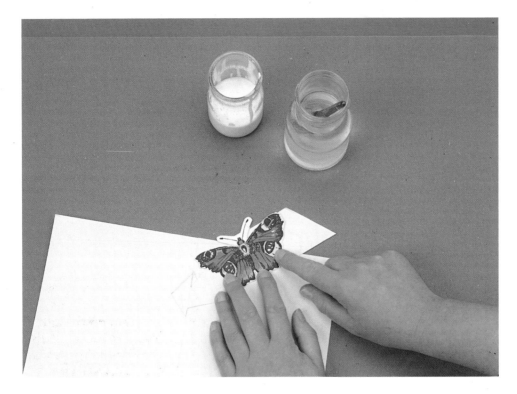

9 Open up the card again and glue your picture to the strip of card inside. If the card strip is longer than your picture, cut away the extra card.

10 As you open and close the card, your picture will move up...

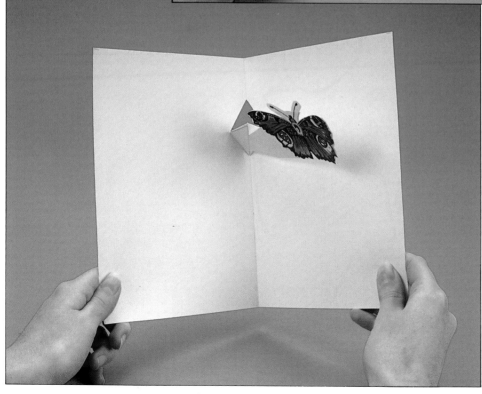

11 ...and down! You could finish off your card by adding some background scenery.

Pop-up pictures

Books with pop-up pictures have been popular since the middle of the 19th century. This idea shows you how to make your own pop-up design. You might like to make a special pop-up card for a special occasion – a surprise birthday card, or even a get well card.

You will need thin white card, felt-tip pens, a pencil, a ruler, scissors, PVA glue and a glue brush.

1 Fold an A4 piece of card in half. Draw a picture (a building or a person) on another, smaller piece of card.

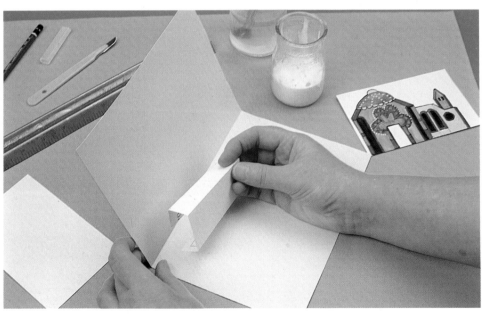

2 Score and fold a strip of card to form a box shape with a rectangular end. Glue this shape into the fold of your card as shown, so that the sides are parallel to the back and the base. Test to see if your card will fold flat, then leave to dry.

3 Cut out your picture and glue it to the front of the folded box shape. Test again to make sure your card will close.

4 You can add to your picture by using another piece of card folded in the same way. Here some trees are being added beside the castle.

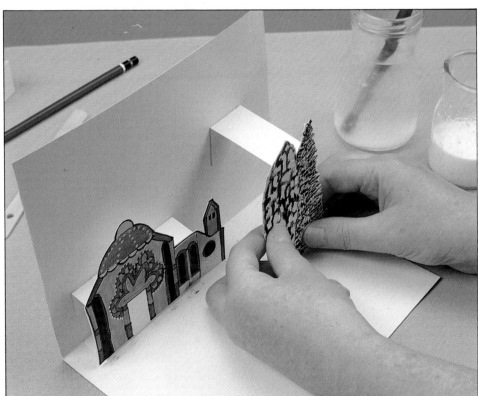

A pop-up toy

This is another pop-up idea to surprise your friends – a figure with a ping-pong ball for a head!

You will need a large plate, some thin fabric, felt-tip pens, scissors, a craft knife, a garden stick (about 30cm long), a ping-pong ball, a needle, coloured card, PVA glue, a glue brush, a yoghurt pot, coloured wrapping paper, an elastic band and wool or ribbon.

1 Use a large plate to help you draw a circle on the fabric. Cut out the circle. This will be the doll's dress.

2 To find the centre of your material circle, fold it in half then in half again. Cut a very small hole at the point of the fold, as shown. Then, using the craft knife, sharpen one end of the garden stick.

3 Draw eyes and a mouth on the ping-pong ball and make a small hole in the bottom with the needle.

4 Draw and cut out two hands with cuffs from a piece of card. Here, a white card template was used. Draw lines on the material circle to mark the position of the hands, as shown. Cut along these lines.

5 Glue the cuffs and push the hands through the cut lines from the inside. Hold to dry. Now push the sharpened stick through the centre hole.

6 Push the pointed end of the stick through the hole in the ping-pong ball. Cover the yoghurt pot with a piece of wrapping paper.

7 Make a small hole in the centre of the base of the pot and push the stick through.

8 Using PVA glue, stick the bottom of the dress to the outside rim of the yoghurt pot. Hold it in place with an elastic band while it dries.

9 Give your doll some hair. Use wool, ribbon, or curled strips of paper. Fix the hair in position with glue.

10 When your doll is dry you can pull it right back into the yoghurt pot.

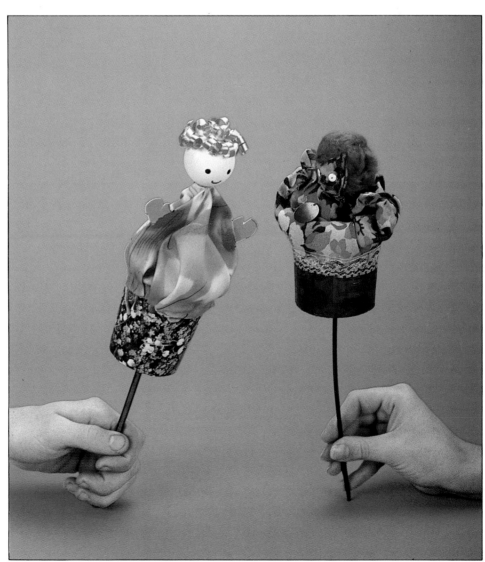

11 What a surprise when your doll pops up!

Making a still picture move

This picture is a rubbed crayon design which gives the impression of movement by repeating the rubbing several times. You will need thin card, a pencil, scissors, PVA glue, a glue brush, heavy card for mounting, paper and crayons.

1 Cut a picture from thin card and glue it to a mounting board. Design your picture in two or three layers. This design shows an early steam engine.

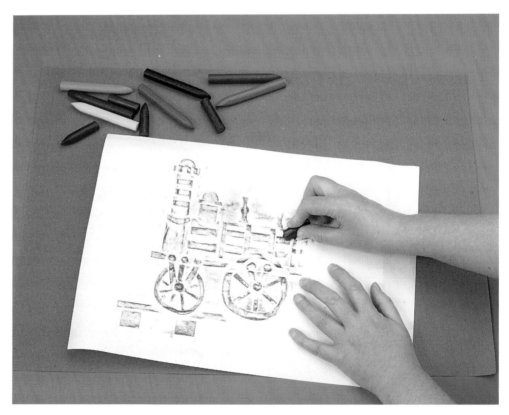

2 Place a sheet of paper over the board and rub across the raised design with the side of a crayon.

3 Move the paper along and make a second and third rubbing. Here the train appears to be slowing down.

4 Many rubbings create the impression of a fast-moving train.

32

5 Here is a clown design. You can see the raised surfaces.

6 A somersaulting clown.

Moving images – a zoetrope

This toy dates from Victorian times. The word 'zoetrope' comes from Greek words meaning 'the wheel of life'. When you spin the zoetrope a series of still pictures appears to move, or come to life!

You will need thin card, a paper plate, scissors, a pencil, a ruler, felt-tip pens, PVA glue, a glue brush, sticky tape, a long pin, a bead, and a bottle with a cork.

1 Cut a length of card about 15cm in height and long enough to fit around the outside edge of a paper plate or cake board. (You may have to join two lengths of card together.)

2 Draw and cut slits evenly along the top of the length of card, as shown. These slits should be about 5cm deep and 1cm wide. Draw a line 1.5cm above the bottom edge of the card.

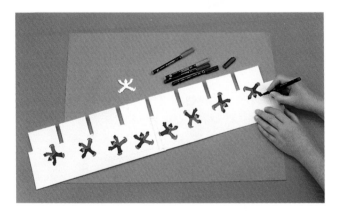

3 Draw a figure between and below each slit. Each figure should be in a slightly different positon. Here a clown is doing a somersault in eight progressive movements.

4 Make small triangular cuts along the bottom edge of the length of card and up to the drawn line.

5 Fold up the tabs you have made then...

6 ...glue them around the outside rim of the paper plate. Fix firmly with tape.

7 Push the long pin through the centre of the plate. Thread the bead on to the pin before pushing it vertically into the cork in the bottle.

8 Holding the bottle firmly with one hand, spin the zoetrope and look through the slits. You will see your figure move.

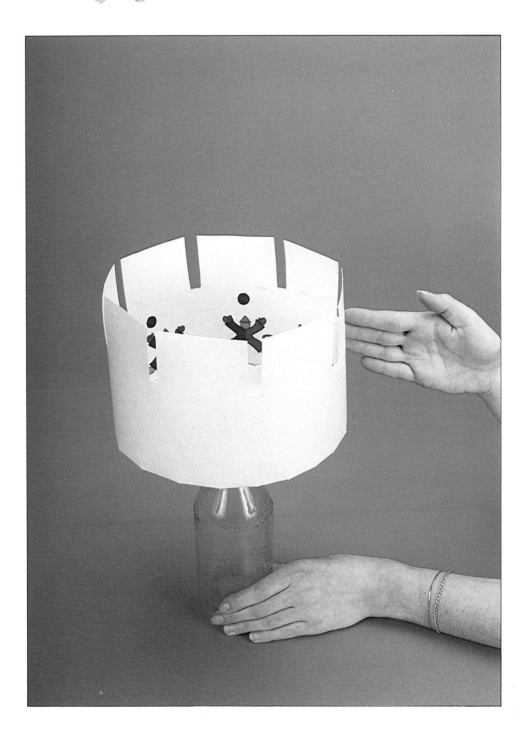

You can make other picture strips to fit inside your zoetrope. Here are some suggestions:

a) a juggler,
b) a runner,
c) a jumping horse.

Moving images – a flick book

This is another optical illusion. When you flick the pages of this book, the dot will appear to move.

You will need paper, card, a pencil, a ruler, scissors, a felt-tip pen, and glue.

1 Cut thirty pieces of paper and two pieces of card, each 5cm wide and 10cm long. The card will be the book cover, and the paper will be the pages. Draw a line 4cm from one end of each page.

2 Using a felt-tip pen, draw a dot on the first page. Place the next page on top of the first so that you can see the dot through the page. Draw a dot on this second page so that it is in a slightly different position from the first.

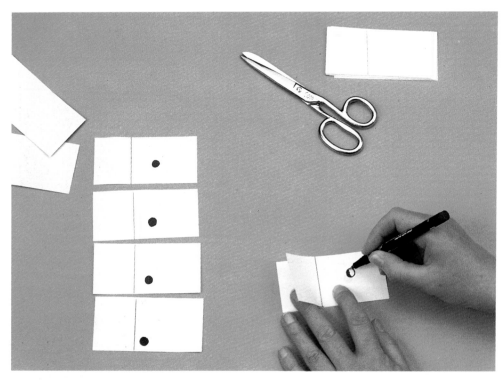

3 Continue to make a dot on each page in the same way, so that each new dot moves slightly away from the one on the previous page. Place the pages in order, as shown.

4 When you have made a dot on each of the thirty pages, work back from the last page to the first (remembering to keep the pages in order), and glue each page together on the other side of the line.

5 Glue a card cover on both sides of your book. Leave to dry. Hold the book in one hand and flick through the pages with the other. The dot will appear to move.

Using the same technique, you could try to make a person move by drawing a slightly differently positioned figure on each page.

A circular spinner

This is another idea which shows how a picture can remain in the 'mind's eye' even after it has disappeared. It is called a thaumatrope, from Greek words meaning 'spinning wonder'.

You will need card, a pair of compasses, a pencil, scissors, white paper, felt-tip pens, glue, a needle and thread.

1 Cut out two circles of card, each with a 5cm radius. Draw two circles, also with a 5cm radius, on a piece of paper. Draw a person in one of the paper circles.

2 Cut out the circle with the person in it and place it *underneath* the other paper circle so that the picture shows through. Draw the frame of a house on the *top* circle, so that the person appears to be standing inside. Mark the top and bottom of both pictures with a dot.

3 Cut out the second paper circle and colour both pictures. Mount each picture on one of the card circles, for support.

4 Matching the dots top and bottom, glue the pictures back to back so that one of the pictures is upside-down.

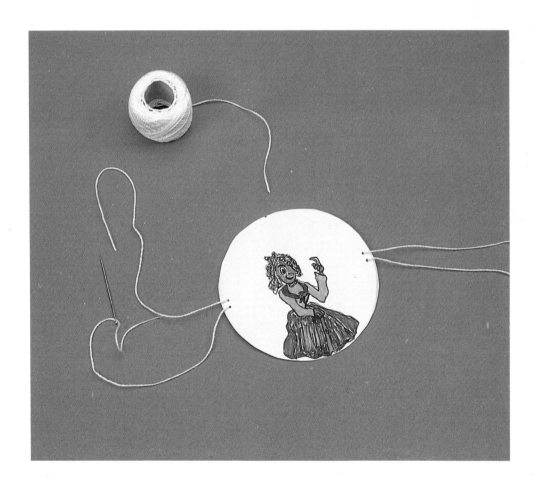

5 Using the needle, make two holes on either side of your spinner. Thread cotton through each side. Tie the ends.

6 Hold the spinner by the threads and swing it to twist the threads. As the threads rapidly unwind, the person will appear to be standing in the house! This happens because you see the second picture before your eye has forgotten the first.

Try to design some other thaumatrope pictures of your own. Here are some ideas
a)   a bird in a tree,
b)   a mouse in a hole,
c)   a bee in a hive.

A twirling snake

To make a colourful spinning snake you will need a small plate, white card, a pen or pencil, felt-tip pens, scissors, and a needle and thread.

1 Use the small plate to help you draw a circle on a piece of card. Draw a spiral line inside the circle to the centre.

2 Draw the head of a snake at the centre, then decorate the snake's body with felt-tip pens.

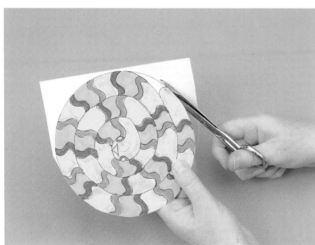

3 Cut out the snake and...

4 ...cut carefully around the spiral.

5 Using the needle, pull a length of cotton thread through the centre of the snake's head. Tie a knot at the end of the cotton so that it does not pull through.

6 If you hang your snake over a warm radiator, the snake will spin. It moves in the current of rising warm air. (The snake on the left has been decorated with coloured sequins.)

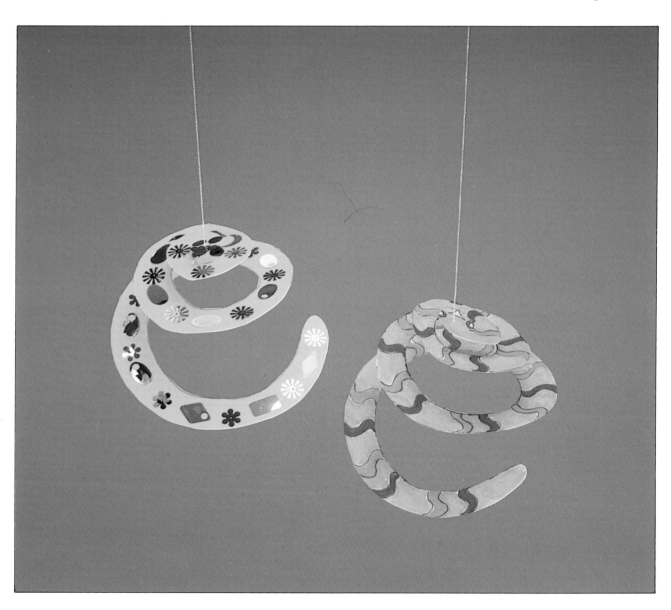

A twirling doll

This doll is called a 'poupard' doll. Its name comes from French words meaning 'doll without legs'. Simple examples were made long ago using a wooden ball on a stick. This was wrapped in cloth to represent a baby doll.

To make a poupard doll you need a plastic bowl, wallpaper paste and water, newspaper, a dowel rod, PVA glue, a glue brush, ribbons, thread, paints, a paintbrush, wool, a needle and beads.

1 Mix a small quantity of wallpaper paste in the plastic bowl. Tear some newspaper into small pieces, and drop these into the paste. Stir well until the papier mâché mixture is stiff enough to mould into a ball shape for the doll's head.

2 When you have made the head, hold it in one hand and push the dowel rod inside, almost to the top. Remove the rod, and leave the head to dry.

3 Glue about six coloured ribbons to the rod at the place where the neck will be. Secure with thread.

4 When the head is dry, paint the head and the face.

5 Glue the dowel rod into the head. Attach some wool for hair, and sew beads to the ends of the ribbons.

45

6 As you twirl the doll, the beads will swing out on the ribbons.

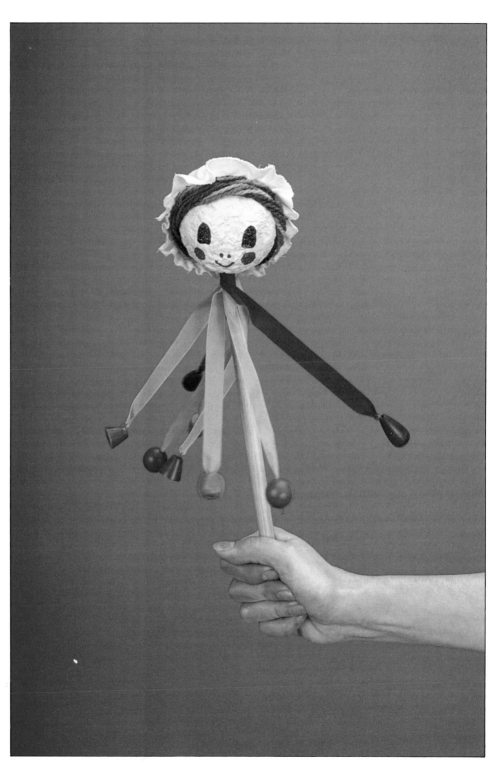

You could use bells instead of beads to make a musical doll.

On your own

1 An assortment of junk materials.

A walking fantasy creature
Here is a chance to be really imaginative and creative! You can use an assortment of junk materials such as paper plates, old boxes, cardboard tubes and fabric scraps. You will also need paints, two matchboxes, some modelling clay, two strips of thick card, a hole punch, thin string and glue.

First, make a body from a cardboard box or tube. Use a paper plate, card lid or paper cone for the head. (The head and body can be any shape you like. You choose!) Decorate your figure with paint.

Make two feet from matchboxes filled with modelling clay. This will make them heavy. Join the head to the body with a strip of material, and the feet to the body with string. Punch a hole at each end of the two card strips. Glue them together to make a cross shape.

2 Join the head, body and 'knees' of your fantasy creature to the card cross. As you lift each leg and swing the heavy feet forward, your creature will walk!

Most of the materials mentioned in this book are easy to obtain.

Make your own collection of assorted waste materials (e.g. old boxes, waste packaging, scraps of material) and store them in a large box. Once you start looking, you will find all sorts of interestingly shaped cardboard packets and tubes!

Ping-pong balls are inexpensive if you purchase practice balls.

Paper and card
Most stationers stock a good range of paper and card in different weights, textures and colours.

Specialist materials
Specialist materials such as oil pastels, beads, and sequins, can be obtained from the larger department stores, artists' materials stockists, or ordered through a schools' supplier such as Nottingham Educational Supplies, Ludlow Hill Road, West Bridgeforth, Nottingham, NG2 6HD.

Adhesives
Cold water paste (e.g. wallpaper paste) is suitable for sticking papers and lightweight materials. Acrylic PVA adhesives (e.g. Alocryl or Marvin) are suitable for heavier materials. For a more instant, quick-drying glue try Bostik Solvent-Free, UHU glue or Copydex.
ON NO ACCOUNT SHOULD IMPACT ADHESIVES BE USED.

Acrylic PVA adhesive can also be mixed with powder paint to produce an acrylic paint. This will give a shiny, more lasting finish to a painted model.

Scoring card
In order to fold a piece of card along a straight line it is easier if you score the card first. Place a metal ruler along the line to be scored and make a firm cut with a craft knife. Do not cut through the card. It will then be easy to fold your card along the line.